JAMES JOYCE IN 90 MINUTES

James Joyce
IN 90 MINUTES

Paul Strathern

IVAN R. DEE
CHICAGO

www.ivanrdee.com

Library of Congress Cataloging-in-Publication Data:
Strathern, Paul, 1940–
    James Joyce in 90 minutes / Paul Strathern.
       p. cm.
    Includes bibliographical references and index.
    ISBN 1-56663-649-3 (cloth : alk. paper) —
    ISBN 1-56663-648-5 (pbk. : alk. paper)
    1. Joyce, James, 1882–1941. 2. Authors, Irish—
20th century—Biography. I. Title.
PR6019.O9Z8137 2005
823'.912—dc22

                                            2005007819

Contents

JAMES JOYCE IN 90 MINUTES

Introduction

The writings of James Joyce represent one of the high watermarks of modernism, the cultural movement that swept Europe and the Americas during the first decades of the twentieth century. By the end of the nineteenth century, Western art, in all its forms, had reached a maturity and sophistication that echoed the society out of which it had grown. But in achieving such a civilized veneer, this bourgeois-dominated society had also become staid, stifling, and hypocritical. Unacceptable elements of human behavior, such as our primitive sexuality, instinctive aggression, and the perversities of our imagination were swept under the carpet. Society was beginning to suffocate the very impulses that had caused its dynamic creation.

In 1899, Sigmund Freud published his *Interpretation of Dreams*. The subconscious mind was exposed as a wellspring of unsavory irrationalities which surged beneath the surface of everyday life. Art was not long in reflecting such impulses. In 1907, Picasso painted his strident and terrifying portrait known as *Les Demoiselles d'Avignon*, depicting an array of naked women whose figures were hideously deformed into geometric shapes. This led him to begin painting in the Cubist style, which shattered forever the more realistic or impressionistic visions of previous Western European styles. The relativistic nature of objects in Cubist paintings curiously paralleled the new Theory of Relativity which had recently been proposed by Einstein and would soon bring about a revolution in the world of science. Six years later, in 1913, the world of music underwent a similar convulsion with the performance of Stravinsky's *Rite of Spring*, whose strident discords and rampant primitivism provoked a riot at its first perform-

8

ance in Paris. The artistic world of modernism was born.

All this found its echo in the cataclysm that shook Europe upon the outbreak of the First World War in 1914. The stable and prosperous larger nations of Europe now became locked in an internecine struggle which shattered their smug and stable societies once and for all. In the midst of this war, one of Europe's largest nations, Russia, succumbed to revolution and the formation of an entirely new society under communism. At the end of four long years of war, Europe's most extensive empire, that of Austro-Hungary, simply collapsed, falling apart into a number of distinct nation-states.

During this prolonged period of artistic and social upheaval, several writers had begun composing works that carried modernism beyond art and music into literature and philosophy. By a remarkable coincidence, several of the major works of literary modernism appeared before the public in 1922—it came to be known as the *annus mirabilis* of the new era. The American poet T. S. Eliot, now resident in Britain, published his epic poem *The Waste Land*, a work expressing a modernist yet sophisticated despair. The same year also saw the appearance of the Austrian philosopher Wittgenstein's *Tractatus-Logico-Philosophicus*, which introduced an entirely new philosophical vision whose clarity and logical precision cut through the more ponderous profundities of previous philosophy. But the transcendental work of modernism to appear in this year was undoubtedly James Joyce's *Ulysses*. Here was a work the like of which had never been seen before. The realistic conventions of the mature bourgois novel were smashed forever into a plethora of styles—all laying claim to an entirely new realism, which reflected the entirely new ways in which humanity was coming to regard itself and the world around it. Most characteristic of Joyce's stylistic techniques was his "stream of consciousness" method, depicting all the thoughts, reflections, fantasies, impulses, and dark imaginings that passed through the human mind. Here was Freud's anarchistic unconscious rendered into all manner of literary forms, whose shocking authenticity and realism would provoke outrage. Readers were confronted with a true mirror of their thoughts, and they hypocritically chose not to like what they saw. Here was the underside of human impulses rendered into art. It would take some time before the shocking inventiveness and originality of Joyce's work would be accepted as literature. Like the other seminal works of modernism, this was the art of the future. The twentieth century had found its voice in the work of James Joyce (who punningly referred to himself as "Shame's Voice").

James Joyce's Life and Works

James Joyce was born in Rathgar, a middle-class suburb in south Dublin on February 2, 1882. His mother Mary Jane (known as May) had met his father John Stanislaus Joyce when they were both in the choir of the local Catholic church; music, especially singing, would continue to play a prominent role in Joyce family life. James was the eldest surviving child but would not remain an only child for long, soon acquiring several brothers and sisters. James's father was secretary of the Dublin and Chapelizod Distilling Company; later he became a civil servant in the taxation department.

At the age of six, young James was sent to Clongowes Wood College, a Jesuit boarding school some fifty miles away in County Kildare. This was generally regarded as the finest Catholic school in Ireland. On arrival, young James was asked his age, to which he replied, "Half-past six." From an early age, James exhibited a precocious verbal talent—no mean feat in a nation noted for such talent at all ages. James was young to be sent away as a boarder, even at a time when middle-class children were customarily packed off early to boarding school; as a result he suffered from homesickness, but he was quickly chided out of this, as was the manner of the time. He was soon participating in the usual rough and tumble of boarding-school life, to the point where the priest in charge of the pupils' health remarked in a letter to James's mother: "He is very well—his face being, as usual, very often well marked with any black thing that comes within reach." James's precocious intellect soon began manifesting itself in an eye for detail and a love of sorting things in order, causing his father to observe admiringly, "If that fellow was dropped in the middle of the Sahara, he'd sit, be God, and make a map of it."

Then disaster struck. In 1892, James's father lost his job in the tax department, and his tendency to a certain fecklessness now became pronounced. From this time on he was never able to find regular employment, taking on various temporary and part-time jobs, including work soliciting advertisements for a Dublin newspaper. Owing to the rapid decline in family fortunes, James was withdrawn from Clongowes Wood College after just three years. For the next two years he would remain at home, largely educating himself, with a little help from his hard-pressed but sympathetic mother. After thirteen years of marriage she would find herself looking after a household of ten children, with dwindling support from her husband, who now spent more and more of his time in the pubs of Dublin. When he returned home he would sometimes be violent toward May, and on one occasion the teenage James was forced to pin him to the ground while his mother fled to the refuge of a neighbor. During James's teenage years the family was forced to move from their home, then moving became a more regular occurrence, with the family occasionally resorting to a "moonlight flit" to avoid paying the rent. As they moved from house to house, the next always poorer than the last, James became intimately acquainted with one Dublin district after another.

At the age of eleven, James had been sent with his brother Stanislaus to Belvedere College in Dublin, a school run by Jesuits where fees were not required. Here he again shone and was eventually elected head of the Marian Society, the equivalent of head boy. Despite this, he remained an object of suspicion to his Jesuit teachers. He was thought to have lost his faith, and by the time he left Belvedere his doubts about the existence of a Catholic God were beginning to harden. But this was no easy lapse. James's intellect had taken a highly spiritual inclination under the tutelage of the Jesuits, and he spent many long nights of the soul before coming to terms with his loss of faith in his own fashion. He had begun to write poetry, and art now began to take the place of religion in his spiritual life. He took his new vocation very seriously. As he explained to his brother Stanislaus in all earnestness: "There is a certain resemblance between the mystery of the mass and what I am trying to do. I mean that I am trying in my poems to give people some kind of intellectual pleasure or spiritual enjoyment by converting the bread of everyday life into something that has a permanent artistic life of its own." In one way or another, this would remain Joyce's artistic credo throughout the years to come.

In 1898, Joyce entered University College, Dublin, the city's Catholic university. This had opened just a half-century earlier, with high hopes of rivaling the ancient Protestant Trinity College, Dublin, alma mater of a long line of distinguished Anglo-Irish figures, including Oscar Wilde and the philosopher Bishop Berkeley. During the preceding decade the poet Gerald Manley Hopkins had been professor of ancient Greek at University College, but by the time Joyce arrived the Jesuit staff were already imposing a rigid Catholic orthodoxy, and an air of mediocrity prevailed. Nominally Joyce studied English, French, and Italian, but though he read widely in these languages he put in few appearances at lectures. His Jesuit professor of English eccentrically believed that Francis Bacon had written the plays of Shakespeare; Joyce was more interested in who was writing contemporary plays. When he was just eighteen he wrote a long review of Ibsen's final play *When We Dead Awaken*. This he extended into an eight-thousand-word review of Ibsen's entire work, which concluded with a bold psychological study of the controversial Norwegian playwright himself. Perceptively, Joyce noted that although Ibsen was

> . . . an eminently virile man, there is a curious admixture of the woman in his nature. His marvellous accuracy, his faint traces of femininity, his delicacy of swift touch, are perhaps attributable to this admixture. But that he knows women is an incontrovertible fact. He appears to have sounded them to almost unfathomable depths.

The article was accepted by the prestigious, London-based *Fortnightly Review*, where its appearance was the cause of some admiration and not a little jealousy in literary Dublin. It also came to the notice of the aging Ibsen himself, who wrote Joyce a letter of thanks. Later, Joyce wrote a long letter to Ibsen on the occasion of his seventy-third birthday, translating his own English into Norwegian. In this Joyce claimed that "Ireland has produced nothing but a whine to the literature of Europe." This was a controversial opinion of a rich centuries-old tradition which had culminated in his contemporaries Wilde, Shaw, and Yeats. But Joyce had a very pertinent point here. This great Irish literary tradition consisted almost entirely of Anglo-Irish or Protestant writers, who were mainly middle or upper class. There was nothing Anglo about Joyce. He was a Celt, who came from the majority Catholic background, and he no longer subscribed to middle-class mores. What he sought to establish was a *real* Irish tradition, produced by its indiginous Celtic people. He continued his letter to Ibsen by confidently saluting his literary hero:

Your work on earth draws to a close and you are near the silence. It is growing dark for

19

you. . . . You have only opened the way—though you have gone as far as you could upon it. . . . As one of the younger generation for whom you have spoken I give you greeting—not humbly, because I am obscure and you in the glare, not sadly because you are an old man and I am a young man, not presumptuously nor sentimentally. . . .

Joyce was not diffident in implying that he was the man who would one day go farther along the way that Ibsen had opened and "gone as far as you could."

As is often the case with psychological insight, Joyce's characterization of the feminine in Ibsen's nature had more than a touch of the autobiographical about it. Joyce's perception was imbued with a feminine delicacy of touch. But his assertion that Ibsen had "sounded the almost unfathomable depths" of female nature was autobiographical in a very different way. Joyce's early religiosity, along with the sexual repression that pervaded Irish society, had left him with a deeply ambivalent relationship to his own sexuality. He was at the same time highly sexed and highly repressed. This led him to develop a distinctly perverse obsession with intimate bodily odors, a fetish he would retain for the rest of his life.

Joyce's normal sexual appetites eventually found release through encounters with prostitutes in Dublin's "Nighttown," a district frequented mainly by sailors and "tommies" from the British army garrisoned in the country to suppress the Irish independence movement. These sexual encounters left Joyce with a deep sense of shame, arising from his repressive Catholic education by the Jesuits, whose celibacy induced a horror of sex. Yet on a more conscious level Joyce knew himself well enough to recognize his own needs. He wanted sex, and if he wanted to become a complete artist he had to complete his experience. His insights into Ibsen's knowledge of women were in many ways his justification to himself of his sexual encounters with prostitutes. These were necessary for him, both as an artist and as a man—despite the deep undertow of shame that such acts induced. If repressed Ireland prevented

21

him from knowing the unfathomable depths that he felt sure women possessed, he could at least take a step in the direction that Ibsen had taken.

Like many a student, especially in Dublin, Joyce drank more Guinness than he could handle. He preferred the company of medical students, renowned for their hard drinking and Rabelaisian behavior. Anecdotes tell of Joyce being returned home "curled up in a cab like a tobacco spit." In the daytime his visits to lectures were rare; instead he spent hours on end in the National Library, which was just down the street. Here he read far and wide, following the serendipity of his imagination, acquiring a deep knowledge of the world's literature and philosophy as well as a vast accumulation of intellectual trivia, phrases from esoteric languages, obscure sayings, and minor historical facts.

He also continued writing poetry, but now he also began experimenting with poetic prose pieces, which he called "epiphanies"—a theological term referring to a heightened sense of consciousness in which a vision of the godhead or religious revelation takes place. For Joyce, the revelation was spiritual, though expunged of any religious content or sacred meaning. His epiphanies could occur in a vision of "the soul of the commonest object . . . in the vulgarity of speech or of gesture or in a memorable phase of the mind itself." This was a vision of the art and the meaning that lurks in the everyday world, waiting for the artist to apprehend it and discover its radiant truth—an experience which both inspires in him, and is in itself, a heightened sense of consciousness.

In June 1902, Joyce took his final exams, gaining a distinctly ordinary degree with the minimum of effort. His attitude is summed up in the following conversation, which is said to have taken place during his English oral exams:

EXAMINER: How is poetic justice exemplified in the play of *King Lear*?

JOYCE: (*apparently bored*) I don't know.

EXAMINER: Oh come, Mr. Joyce, you are not fair to yourself.

JOYCE: Oh yes, but I don't understand your question. The phrase "poetic justice" is unmeaning jargon so far as I am concerned.

This episode aptly encapsulates both his arrogance and his originality at this early stage of his development. Joyce was now determined to become a writer and equally determined to break free from the stifling parochialism of Dublin. But to do this he realized he would need a job to support himself—so he decided he would become a doctor. He borrowed money from his friends and in December set off with high hopes for Paris. He would study medicine and at the same time write in the capital city of the artistic world. All this was little more than an impractical dream, but it took him to Paris. The study of medicine was soon abandoned in favor of his usual habits. Days of reading in the Sainte-Geneviève Library were followed by nights consuming prodigious amounts of cheap red wine and occasional encounters with prostitutes. In between times he starved, waiting for letters containing money sent by his long-suffering friends.

24

He lived in a small room in the cheap Hôtel Corneille, which in his letters home to his sick and worried mother became transformed into "Le Grand Hotel Corneille." After just four months he received word that his mother was dying and hurried back to her bedside in Dublin. A few months later she was dead.

Joyce now took on various jobs in Dublin, including a four-month stint as a teacher at a private school in Dalkey, south of Dublin. His difficult relationship with his father continued, as his father spent what little money he had on drink, condemning his family to penury. Joyce no longer lived at home, putting up at various addresses with his friends. For a brief period of ten days he lodged with the writer Oliver St. John Gogarty who was living in the Martello Tower by the sea at Sandycove. In the midst of all this Joyce began writing a novel called *Stephen Hero*, whose central character, Stephen Dedalus, was largely based on the spiritual progress of Joyce himself and his epiphanic formative experiences. In 1904 the writer George Russell (better known by his pseudonym

"AE") offered to publish a series of short stories by Joyce at £1 each in the journal he was editing. This was the *Irish Homestead*, whose readership consisted largely of farmers and country people. Joyce published three stories under the pseudonym Stephen Dedalus before it became clear that the blatant realism of his writing was unsuitable for such an audience. Russell rejected his story *Clay*, which described a cousin of Joyce's, thinly disguised as "Maria," who worked in the Dublin by Lamplight laundry, which was in fact an institution providing employment for reformed prostitutes. Despite Russell's rejection, these stories marked Joyce's coming-of-age as a writer.

At the same time Joyce underwent an experience that would mark his coming-of-age as a man—an experience he would celebrate as the most important in his life. On June 10, 1904, as he was walking down Nassau Street in central Dublin, he noticed a young woman with striking red hair. On the spur of the moment he introduced himself to her and asked her out. This was Nora Barnacle, from Galway, who had run away from her home in the west of Ireland and was now working as a chambermaid in the small Finn's Hotel. Nora was struck by Joyce's blue eyes, and the fact that he was wearing a yachting cap made her think he must be a sailor. She was an independent spirit and jauntily agreed to meet him—but later thought better of it. When she didn't turn up, Joyce was crestfallen; he sent her a note, asking for another date "if you have not forgotten me." They met again on Thursday June 16, which Joyce would one day transform into the most famous date in twentieth-century literature. During the course of their evening walk together at Ringsend, a drab suburb at the mouth of the river Liffey, the twenty-two-year-old Joyce must have had the first inkling that Nora was the woman he had been looking for. She was bright, self-confident, yet uneducated. To anyone else she might have seemed distinctly ordinary; but this was part of her attraction to Joyce, along with her native wit and forthright, unaffected character. She appeared both knowing and yet innocent, both mocking and affectionate, in a way that he had never encountered.

27

For all his intellect and apparent self-confidence, Joyce remained essentially a buttoned-up personality, incapable of expressing himself fully except on paper. And even there, his self-exposure was disguised by art. Nora was the first person to penetrate his formidable intellectual defences. Likewise, her curious combination of brazenness and innocence drew him to her in a way he had never felt before with a woman. The nineteen-year-old Nora was still a virgin, yet as they embraced she slipped her hand into his trousers, slowly coaxing him to orgasm while looking at his face with her "quiet saint-like eyes."

From that day on, Joyce wanted to know everything about Nora. They found they had more in common than they might have expected. Her father, a baker, had brought his family to ruin through drink, much like Joyce's father. And she had run away from home, much as Joyce wanted to escape far from his own home and city. Yet despite falling in love, Joyce continued drinking and even got himself involved in a late-night fight over a woman he had propositioned in St. Stephen's Green. After the fight, which resulted in a black eye for Joyce, he was looked after by a Jewish acquaintance called Alfred Hunter, another experience that would assume deep significance in his mind. But Joyce's father appeared to regard his son's antics as a joke. When he heard that Joyce was enamored of a girl with the name of Nora Barnacle, he quipped, "She'll never leave him."

By the autumn Joyce had conceived of a plan to run away with Nora. He proposed this to her, and she accepted. He did not propose marriage because he boldly did not believe in such bourgeois customs. Even more boldly, Nora agreed. On October 9, 1904, just four months after they had first met, Joyce and Nora boarded a boat from Dublin. Joyce had a vague offer of a teaching job at the Berlitz school in Zurich, but this turned out to be spurious. In the end, after many mishaps and last-minute importunings of cash from virtual strangers, Joyce managed to find employment at the Berlitz school in the Adriatic port of Pola, on the tip of the Istrian peninsula in what was then an outpost of the Austro-Hungarian Empire (now part of Croatia). This quickly proved a disappointment. As Joyce wrote to his brother Stanislaus, who had now become his confidant, helpmate, and hapless agent for extorting money from long-suffering friends: "Istria is a long boring place wedged into the Adriatic peopled by ignorant Slavs who wear little red caps and colossal breeches."

Here Joyce and Nora embarked on the adventure of getting to know each other under close domestic circumstances, and in between teaching Joyce tried to write. Although he had always accepted Nora's lack of interest in the arts, he was nonetheless disappointed when he discovered that this lack of interest also extended to *his* art: "Though I am quietly disillusioned I have not been able to discover any falsehood in this nature which had the courage to trust me." It is difficult to judge who was the more daring and gullible of the two. But they managed to survive their escapade together, with the inevitable arguing and making up involved in a relationship between two such disparate but spirited characters.

30

In 1905 they moved fifty miles north to the more cosmopolitan and congenial port of Trieste, where Joyce managed to persuade his brother Stanislaus to join them. Stanislaus duly arrived, took up a teaching post to provide extra money for the family, and began acting as his brother's keeper while domestic circumstances took a dramatic turn for the worse: Joyce and Nora began fighting. Nora by now had two children in quick succession, and Joyce had returned to his old drinking habits. Nights were spent carousing and singing in the cheap sailor bars until he was thrown out and Stanislaus carried him home.

In the midst of all this bohemian squalor, Joyce amazingly continued to write and to read widely in modern European literature. The two main contesting literary movements of the period were realism and symbolism. Joyce found himself equally taken with both, and proceeded to form his own synthesis. Although his style would undergo vast and myriad transformations throughout his career, his basic adherence to these two schools would persist. Joyce's writing would, after its own fashion, remain utterly realistic in its telling detail and vivid evocation of the particular, yet at the same time these details would increasingly be infused with a telling symbolic meaning—to the point where symbol and reality became one.

For the time being Joyce continued writing stories with the Dublin setting he remembered with such fond distaste. The atmospheres he conjured up were intended to illustrate all that was provincial and repressive about the city where he had lived and grown up. The characters he portrayed struggle to escape into some freer and more fulfilling life. Indicatively, the word "life" appears again and again in these stories. On the other hand, Joyce does not believe in the writer telling the reader what he or she should think about the lives that are being described. We are left to judge for ourselves. But the apparently objective prose—always in the third person—frequently takes on the manner of the character it is describing. Likewise the reported conversations are faithfully idiomatic, utterly authentic in tone. All this enables the reader to identify sympathetically with the characters, yet at the same time remain at a distance, allowing a space for both irony and reaction. In allowing the reader to feel more deeply the life of his characters, Joyce enables the reader to understand them—an understanding that undermines any simple judgment he or she might wish to impose.

As Joyce added to these stories, their range extended, expanding into a wider variety of social situations. Each of these is explored with suggestive subtlety. An apparently simple story such as "After the Races" describes a night on the town shared by a young Irishman and his more sophisticated foreign cronies. Joyce deftly implies that the young Irishman, Doyle, is out of his depth with these foreigners—socially, psychologically, and financially—just as provincial Ireland is no match for the sophistications of France, Hungary, England, and America. As we read on, and the evening progresses from drunken toasts in the private room of an expensive restaurant to card-playing on the American's yacht in Kingstown harbor, our unease deepens.

33

But there is no obvious disaster. The story ends with the last card game, at which Doyle has lost heavily, but not more heavily than he can afford.

> He knew that he would regret in the morning but at present he was glad of the rest, glad of the dark stupor that would cover up his folly. He leaned his elbows on the table and rested his head between his hands, counting the beats of his temples. The cabin door opened and he saw the Hungarian standing in a shaft of grey light:
> —Daybreak, gentlemen!

Joyce declared that he intended these stories to be a "chapter of the moral history of my country." Such ambition is frequently evident. In "Two Gallants," Joyce depicts a street musician playing a harp, a common sight in Dublin.

> . . . a harpist stood in the roadway, playing to a little ring of listeners. He plucked at the wires heedlessly, glancing quickly from time to time at the face of each new-comer and from time to time, wearily also, at the sky. His

34

JAMES JOYCE'S LIFE AND WORKS

harp too, heedless that her covering had fallen about her knees, seemed weary alike of the eyes of strangers and of her master's hands. One hand played in bass the melody of Silent, O Moyle, while the other hand careered in the treble after each group of notes. The notes of the air throbbed deep and full.

The two men walked up the street without speaking, the mournful music following them.

The harp is a national symbol of Ireland, and by giving the instrument a gender (in the manner of a ship) he alludes to his naked exploited country, its profound music accompanied by tinkling trills. But Joyce's burgeoning skill is demonstrated in more than somewhat overreaching symbolism. With just a few words he is capable of evoking complex social tensions with immense precision. Here we see Lenehan, the aging gallant, enter a workers' café:

He spoke roughly in order to belie his air of gentility for his entry had been followed by a pause of talk. His face was heated. To appear natural he pushed his cap back on his head and planted his elbows on the table. The mechanic and the two work-girls examined him point by point before resuming their conversation in a subdued voice.

Joyce says neither too much nor too little, and neither too much nor too little happens. These stories are filled with commonplace scenes in which practically nothing takes place, yet with a precision which suggests volumes. Joyce the heavy drinker was no boor; these stories are the work of an extremely sensitive literary artist, alert to every nuance of social behavior. Yet unlike the masters he so admired—such as Ibsen and Flaubert—Joyce's similar, almost feminine sensitivity is applied to the dour realities of Dublin.

The final story of the *Dubliners* collection, "The Dead," was completed in 1907. This was of novella length and brought to a conclusion the underlying theme of the previous stories: the constrictive nature of the life lived by the Dubliners he describes. Yet "The Dead" is far from an exclusively depressive work. It opens with the bustle of guests arriving at the front door, their coats being taken by the maid.

> It was always a great affair, the Misses Morkan's annual dance. Everyone who knew them came to it, members of the family, old friends of the family, the members of Julia's choir, any of Kate's pupils that were grown up enough, and even some of Mary Jane's pupils too. Never once had it fallen flat.

As the narrator's voice describes the hostesses and guests at the party, we become aware of the social layers underlying what is happening. We see Gabriel Conroy, an intellectual journalist and teacher, together with his beautiful wife Greta, a poorly educated woman from Galway, of whom he is highly possessive. These are evidently based upon Joyce and Nora, but the nuances of Gabriel's feelings go far beyond the merely autobiographical. After the party, when Gabriel and Greta are going to bed in their hotel room, she reveals that back in Galway she had once been loved by a young man called Michael Furey, who is now dead. With immense subtlety and resonance, Joyce evokes the complicated feelings that this revelation provokes in Gabriel. He lies in bed beside his sleeping wife, aware of the "wayward and flickering existence . . . [of] the vast hosts of the dead." He begins to feel that "the solid world itself, which these dead had one time reared and lived in, was dissolving and dwindling." In a masterly evocation, these dead and their continuing effect on the living become associated with the snow that is falling outside the window and all over Ireland:

> It was falling on every part of the dark central plain, on the treeless hills, falling softly upon the Bog of Allen and, further westwards, softly falling into the dark mutinous Shannon waves. It was falling, too, upon every part of the lonely churchyard on the hill where Michael Furey lay buried. It lay thickly drifted on the crooked crosses and headstones, on the spears of the little gate, on the barren thorns. His soul swooned slowly

as he heard the snow falling faintly through the universe and faintly falling, like the descent of their last end, upon all the living and the dead.

In 1909 Joyce traveled back to Dublin, attempting to find a publisher for *Dubliners*. But his efforts remained fruitless. The stories were based upon blends of real and recognizable Dublin characters, while the locales they visited were also all too real, sometimes in an almost libelous sense. Joyce had not been sparing in his attempt to convey the truth of what he knew, and all this was too close to the bone for any publisher of the time.

At the same time Joyce became involved in a commercial venture, which he hoped would provide him with some much needed income while he continued with his writing. He managed to interest four businessmen from Trieste in a scheme to open a string of cinemas in Dublin, then in Cork and Belfast. The new "silent movies" were now sweeping the Continent, and Joyce felt sure that this modern form of entertainment could not fail in Ireland. On a second visit to Dublin late in 1909, he opened the Volta Cinema, the first moving picture theatre in the land. It was housed in modest premises on Mary Street, just off the main thoroughfare of Sackville Street (now O'Connell Street). The venture, however, proved nothing but a headache for Joyce, and when he left Dublin to return to Trieste, the Volta soon descended into a money-losing proposition, and was sold. As ever, Joyce's finances remained in a farcical state. In order to obtain a ticket for passage, he would borrow money. On arrival he would then write a fierce letter of complaint to the transport company (rail, ferry, or whatever) demanding a refund and a ticket to return him to his original destination. Larger financial schemes to import firework rockets and homespun Irish tweed to Trieste proved equally fruitless and even more financially painful for his investors.

It was during one of his 1909 trips to Dublin that Joyce heard a piece of unpleasant gossip from a friend. Apparently during the summer of

1904, when Joyce had first been in love with Nora, she had also been seeing someone else. Like Gabriel in "The Dead," Joyce was a possessive partner, prone to suspicions about Nora as well as gnawing bouts of jealousy. This piece of news spurred Joyce to get hopelessly drunk. Fortunately he ran into an old university pal, John Byrne, who carried him back to Byrne's house. Even when Byrne informed Joyce that the gossip about Nora was a demonstrable lie, Joyce continued to harbor the feeling that Nora had betrayed him. This theme of betrayal, which had already occurred as a generating force in "The Dead," would flower into full bloom in his later fiction.

Having completed his objective stories, Joyce now returned to his more overtly subjective novel, recounting the experiences of Stephen Dedalus as he undergoes the transformation from child to renegade youth to more mature young literary artist on the point of leaving his native land to pursue his creative life in exile. *A Portrait of the Artist as a Young Man* opens in a fairy-tale prose intended to convey the timeless world and artless innocence of babyhood:

> Once upon a time and a very good time it was there was a moocow coming down along the road and this moocow that was coming down along the road met a nicens little boy named baby tuckoo. . . .
>
> His father told him that story: his father looked at him through a glass: he had a hairy face.
>
> He was baby tuckoo. . . .

Such is the subtlety of Joyce's telling that he manages to have it all ways. This is how it feels to be a baby. Yet it is also the father telling the story. At the same time it is the objective narrative voice.

With uncanny accuracy, Joyce evokes the perceptions of childhood:

> When you wet the bed first it is warm then it gets cold. His mother put on the oilsheet. That had the queer smell.
>
> His mother had a nicer smell than his father.

It quickly becomes clear that in *Portrait* Joyce has moved on from the more realistic form of *Dubliners*. This enables him to be both more loose and more experimental in style, yet at the same time to organize the structure of the novel in a more formalistic fashion. The narrative progresses in episodic form through Stephen's spiritual growth and the constricting society that seeks to confine him. The flow of Stephen's developing artistic temperament comes up against the founding rocks on which Irish society is built: the family, the Roman Catholic church, and the Irish nationalist movement. Each of these, in its own way, threatens to stifle his spirit.

Stephen's life follows faithfully that of his author. We see him at Clongowes Wood, at Belvedere College, and later at University College, Dublin. The incidents recounted all clearly reflect those experienced by Joyce. Yet it would be a mistake to suppose that Stephen Dedalus is intended merely as a faithful self-portrait. As the title implies, this is a portrait of "the artist." Many of the ideas about art, which play such a formative role in the development of Stephen's temperament, are borrowed directly from other sources—especially from modern writers such as Yeats, Flaubert, Wilde, and Ibsen. But the central aesthetic theory proposed by Stephen, involving the interplay of Good and Beauty, harks back to that of Thomas Aquinas, the thirteenth-century theologian who played such a leading role in medieval Catholicism. Joyce may have rejected Catholicism, but he recognized its strengths and was willing to use them.

Stephen's struggle and break with Catholicism is recounted in some detail. Interwoven with it is his sensual development and his attitude toward the "sins of the flesh" so abhorred by the church. The high point of this conflict occurs during a retreat, when the schoolboy Stephen listens to the series of sermons delivered by Father Arnall, on such themes as:

Remember only the last things and thou shalt not sin for ever—words taken, my dear little brothers in Christ, from the book of Ecclesiastes, seventh chapter, fortieth verse.

Father Arnall increasingly focuses his attentions upon the pains of hell, which are evoked in some detail:

> In hell all laws are overturned—there is no thought of family or country, of ties, of relationships. The damned howl and scream at one another, their torture and rage intensified by the presence of beings tortured and raging like themselves. All sense of humanity is forgotten. The yells of the suffering sinners fill the remotest corners of the vast abyss.

Nowadays such loving lingering upon these sadistic topics might be taken more as a reflection of the psychology of the sermonizer himself: a transparent window to the sufferings of a celibate seminarian. Although Joyce was certainly aware of such an interpretation, this was not his prime intention. We are focused upon (and share) Stephen's psychological and spiritual reaction to such sermons, which were indeed a commonplace of schoolboy experience at the time:

> He passed up the staircase and into the corridor along the walls of which the overcoats

and waterproofs hung like gibbeted malefactors, headless and dripping and shapeless. And at every step he feared that he had already died, that his soul had been wrenched forth of the sheath of his body, that he was plunging headlong through space.

While he is still a believer, Stephen strives to avoid temptation and sin:

The leprous company of his sins closed about him, breathing upon him, bending over him from all sides. He strove to forget them in an act of prayer, huddling his limbs closer together and binding down his eyelids: but the senses of his soul would not be bound.

The novel comes to a close in a series of diary entries. They are objective in their documentary form yet convey in an abbreviated manner Stephen's deepest worries and aspirations as well as the beginnings of his literary talent. He ends by bidding his farewell to Ireland:

. . . Welcome, O Life! I go to encounter for the millionth time the reality of experience and to forge in the smithy of my soul the uncreated conscience of my race.

April 27th. Old father, old artificer, stand me now and ever in good stead.

Dublin, 1904
Trieste, 1914

The byline marks the beginning and the end of Joyce's struggle as a writer to give the recalcitrant material of his life a suitable artistic form. It also points to the fact that Dublin is now far behind him, in time though not in memory. The intervening years have been spent creating this work as an article of artistic faith rather than one of more immediate autobiography.

The artist, like the God of creation, remains within or behind or beyond or above his handiwork, invisible, refined out of existence, indifferent, paring his fingernails.

Yet this credo requires more than passivity of the artist himself. He must struggle and suffer to

47

attain such Godlike status: Stephen's vow to himself strikes a more personal note:

> I will not serve that in which I no longer believe whether it call itself my home, my fatherland or my church: and I will try to express myself in some mode of life or art as freely as I can and as wholly as I can, using for my defence the only arms I allow myself to use, silence, exile and cunning.

Joyce would experience considerable difficulty in getting *Portrait* published. Its form was too experimental, its subject matter too controversial, and its general attitude too far in advance of its time.

Fortunately, these were just the qualities that appealed to the American poet Ezra Pound, who had taken up residence in London in 1908. Pound had launched himself upon the London literary scene, where he quickly became the noisy self-appointed champion of the new modernism. Yet Pound had much more than a flair for self-publicity: his eye for new talent was unerring. Already he had spotted, and enthusiastically championed, Robert Frost and T. S. Eliot. Joyce sent the manuscript of *Portrait of the Artist as a Young Man* to Pound, who immediately wrote back, declaring the novel to be "damn fine stuff." Pound used his connections, and in February 1914 the influential London literary magazine *The Egoist* began serializing *Portrait*. By now *Dubliners* had also been accepted by a London publisher, and in June 1914 Joyce's stories of his native city were finally published. At last it looked as if his luck had changed.

In August 1914, Europe plunged into the First World War, with Britain and Austro-Hungary on opposing sides. Joyce had no great love of Britain and as an Irishman had decidedly neutral sympathies. The sight of France and Germany, both of whose literatures he loved, declaring war on each other filled him with despair. But Joyce remained technically a British citizen, and his continuing residence in Austro-Hungarian Trieste made him an enemy alien. Nonetheless the Austro-Hungarian authorities astutely calculated that Joyce posed no threat to their military effort, and he was allowed to continue teaching. His brother Stanislaus was not so fortunate; he soon began publicly proclaiming his pro-Italian sympathies, and as a result was interned by the authorities in a camp for enemy aliens.

Joyce himself soon began to realize the potential danger of his situation and obtained a visa for neutral Switzerland. Together with Nora and his two young children, Giorgio and Lucia, he took up residence in Zurich. Joyce now found himself with no pupils to tutor and no source of income, but fortunately Pound used his influence to persuade the Royal Literary Fund in London to send Joyce £15 to see him through until he could find new pupils. Joyce and his family of nomadic exiles settled into their new country as best they could. Nora, who spoke Irish with a heavy Galway accent, and had with difficulty learned to speak German with an all but impenetrable Triestine accent, now set about the formidable task of getting her tongue around Schweitzerdeutsch (the heavily accented Swiss dialect of German spoken in Zurich). As Joyce happily pointed out, Nora now spoke English and two versions of German, none of which were comprehensible to an Englishman or a German. By this time, Joyce prided himself on his ability to make witty conversational puns and sexual innuendos in European languages ranging from Norwegian to ancient Greek.

This linguistic dexterity and sophistication now began to manifest itself in the new, highly ambitious work upon which Joyce embarked. It would succeed in being even more autobiographical yet even more objective than his *Portrait of the Artist as a Young Man*. The objectivity would be achieved by an increasingly daring use of stylistic experimentation, which would be employed to convey all that he could remember of life in Dublin. The novel, which he called *Ulysses*, would be set on June 16, 1904, obliquely celebrating the day on which he first went out with Nora Barnacle. It would open with Stephen Dedalus and Buck Mulligan in the Martello Tower at Sandycove

> Stately, plump Buck Mulligan came from the stairhead, bearing a bowl of lather on which a mirror and a razor lay crossed. A yellow

dressing-gown, ungirdled, was sustained gently behind him by the mild morning air.

Stephen Dedalus is freshly returned from a brief spell of exile in Paris, uncertain of whether he should remain in his native city or leave for more permanent exile. He goes to the private school where he has taught, to collect his wages from the headmaster:

He stood in the porch and watched the laggard hurry towards the scrappy field where sharp voices were in strife. They were sorted in teams and Mr. Deasy came stepping over whisps of grass with gaitered feet. When he reached the schoolhouse voices again contending called to him. He turned his angry white moustache.

—What is it now, he cried continually without listening.

—Cochrane and Halliday are on the same side, sir, Stephen cried.

—Will you wait in my study for a moment, Mr. Deasy said, till I restore order here.

The scenes are recognizably from Joyce's life: his brief stay with Gogarty in the Martello Tower, his period as a teacher in the private school at Dalkey. But it is clear from the above passages that Joyce is not interested in painting any rounded autobiographical pictures. He makes the reader flesh out the scenes with his own imagination, and he does this by concentrating on sharp imagistic details. These are then interspersed with dialogue—or with Stephen's thoughts, as in the next scene where he walks across the strand:

> Ineluctible modality of the visible: at least that if no more, thought through my eyes. Signatures of all things I am here to read, sea-spawn and seawrack, the nearing tide, that rusty boot. Snotgreen, bluesilver, rust: coloured signs. Limits of the diaphane. . . . Stephen closed his eyes to hear his boots crush crackling wrack and shells. You are walking through it howsomever. I am, a stride at a time. A very short space of time through very short times of space.

Joyce wishes to re-create the very consciousness of Stephen—the sense impressions, interspersed with his passing thoughts, and the little trails of association they provoke. We experience the world just as if we are in Stephen's head, seeing through his eyes, listening to the voice of his own consciousness. All this may appear unrealistic and highly fragmentary on the page, but it is only because we are used to a more conventional literary version of reality. Joyce wants to subvert this convention, which is in fact no more "realistic" than any other. His aim is to provoke the reader into imagining a more vivid reality as he reads the words on the page. His intention is to render his words closer to the actuality of individual experience. Such prose is "difficult" only because following the conscious experience of another can be difficult. We have to learn to accept the apparent nonsequiturs of this private personal consciousness— just as we accept with ease the apparent nonsequiturs of our own consciousness. But this was just the beginning, both of the book and of Joyce's aims in writing it.

Joyce would spend his next seven years concentrating upon the increasing complexities of *Ulysses*. He remained in Zurich with his family throughout the war. In 1917 the complete version of *Portrait of the Artist as Young Man* was published in London. Mainstream critics greeted it with bafflement and irritation, one declaring, "It is difficult to know what to say about this new book." Another went so far as to suggest that Joyce would be better off writing "a treatise on drains." But the loyal Ezra Pound came forcefully to his rescue: "Joyce is a writer, GODDAM your eyes." The book also received a complimentary review in the *Times Literary Supplement*, which proclaimed: "It is wild youth, as wild as Hamlet's, and full of wild music." This anonymous review was written by Harriet Weaver, who had taken over as editor of *The Egoist*. Harriet Weaver was an unmarried forty-one-year-old Englishwoman from a rich Quaker background, who quickly conceived an unbounded admiration for Joyce's work. When she heard of his financial plight in Zurich, she immediately set about supporting him. Around this time Joyce began suffering from a series of painful eye diseases which would eventually render him blind in one eye, with his sight severely debilitated in the other. Harriet Weaver now paid for the first of what would become a protracted series of painful and costly operations on Joyce's eyes.

In 1918 the first episodes of *Ulysses* began appearing in *The Little Review*, published in New York. These would continue to appear, to some acclaim in avant-garde circles, until 1920, when *The Little Review* was forced to abandon serialization after it was sued by the New York Society for the Suppression of Vice.

Joyce had now moved to Paris, where he surmised that his writing was more likely to be appreciated. He felt it stimulating to be speaking a new language while the long-suffering Nora did her best to overcome it. The Joyce family had now lived in Pola, Trieste (with a brief interlude in Rome), Zurich, and Paris, with frequent changes of address in each city when trouble arose over the rent. Despite his often difficult or cantankerous social manner, Joyce was a sensitive man; his frequent moving and even more frequent money troubles caused him great suffering. His way out of this was to bury himself in his work. For Nora it was a different matter. She remained very much her own forthright self and was neither willing nor able to appreciate Joyce's work. She saw in him an ordinary man, and loved him for this. Likewise she wished to live an ordinary family life, but this could never be. The two children, Giorgio and Lucia, were now in their early teens and were growing disoriented by all the shuffling around. For them, Paris meant getting to know people in yet another new school and becoming fluent in yet another language. Both of them were developing into increasingly unruly children. Joyce refused to discipline them, and Nora found her task of unaided parenthood more and more difficult.

But in public the Joyces still presented the picture of a united family. Their cheap rooms had no cooking facilities, so they were forced to eat out each night at an inexpensive restaurant called Michaud's, around the corner from where they lived. Here they became one of the sights of the neigborhood, as observed by the young Ernest Hemingway:

> Joyce peering at the menu through his thick glasses, holding the menu up in one hand; Nora by him, a hearty but delicate eater; Giorgio, thin, foppish, sleek-headed from the back; Lucia with heavy curly hair, a girl not quite yet grown; all of them talking Italian.

Not long after Joyce's arrival in Paris, he was introduced to the American Sylvia Beach, who had opened the English-language bookshop Shakespeare and Company. It turned out that Beach was already an admirer of Joyce's work, having followed with great interest the episodes of *Ulysses* as they appeared in *The Little Review*. Joyce now showed her copies of the ensuing episodes. *Ulysses* was by now all but complete, but no English publisher was showing any interest. On the contrary, the court case in New York meant that *Ulysses* was now considered an obscene book. Such an accurate rendering of the flow of human consciousness was regarded as unpublishable. Joyce was in despair when Sylvia

Beach asked him: "Would you let Shakespeare and Company have the honor of bringing out your *Ulysses*?" Joyce accepted her offer "immediately and joyfully." *Ulysses* would finally be published on February 4, 1922, Joyce's fortieth birthday. Copies were put on sale at Sylvia Beach's bookshop and began circulating among expatriate writers in Paris. Ezra Pound was soon smuggling copies to the likes of T. S. Eliot and Virginia Woolf in London while Hemingway concealed copies in his trousers on his way into the United States.

News of this new undergound masterpiece began circulating by word of mouth, and Joyce was soon famous in artistic circles in Paris. Invited to a dinner party for Diaghilev and Stravinsky, he was even introduced to Marcel Proust, the great chronicler of Parisian aristocratic society. According to one report, the meeting between the two greatest writers of their age went as follows:

PROUST: Ah, Monsieur Joyce. Do you know the Princess X [a celebrated aristocrat]?

JOYCE: No, Monsieur.

PROUST: But surely you know the Countess Y [a famous Parisian socialite]?

JOYCE: No, Monsieur.

PROUST: Then you must know Madame Z [a leading society hostess]?

JOYCE: No, Monsieur.

The Dublin that Joyce portrayed in *Ulysses* was a world away from the sophistications of Proust, yet the subtleties that Joyce employed in the telling of his tale were if anything more sophisticated even than Proust's famed sensibility.

Joyce had understood from the beginning that the realistic portrayal of an individual "stream of consciousness" would present more difficulties than the occasional obscenity that such a method would inevitably throw up. The apparent nonsequiturs and obscure associations would produce a hopelessly inartistic jumble, utterly unacceptable to an extremely well-developed aesthetic sensibility such as Joyce's. So how was he to organize all this material into a coherent whole? The clue lies in the apparently inappropriate title. What has Ulysses, the hero of Homer's *Odyssey*, to do with a description of a day in Dublin? Joyce decided to use the episodic narrative of Homer's epic poem as a structure on which to place his own narrative—to give his words a hidden backbone, a direction, an overall coherence. Each of the episodes in Dublin would contain subtle echoes of the appropriate scene in the *Odyssey*.

Homer's epic poem the *Odyssey* originated in ancient Greece around the ninth century B.C. and is one of the founding works of Western literature. Its main story is simply told. It recounts the adventures of Ulysses on his long return voyage from the Trojan Wars on the shore of what is now western Turkey, to his home on the island of Ithaca at the mouth of the Adriatic Sea. This journey would take him ten years and require all his native cunning to elude the many traps placed in his way by the angry sea god Poseidon, whom he has offended. Many of the trials he undergoes take place in mythical locations and involve legendary characters. On his way, Ulysses encounters such figures as the one-eyed Cyclops, the seductive Calypso, and the witch

Circe who turns men into swine. He also manages to survive such physical dangers as the whirlpool and the clashing rocks, Scylla and Charybdis. Finally, he returns to learn that his faithful wife Penelope is beset by pressing suitors who have taken over his palace and seduced many of her serving maids. The suitors plan to murder Ulysses' son Telemachus upon his return from his search for his father. Adopting a disguise, Ulysses slays his wife's suitors as well as her treacherous maidservants before he is eventually united with Penelope.

As we have seen, the opening scene of Joyce's *Ulysses* takes place in the Martello Tower where Stephen Dedalus is confronted by Buck Mulligan and later by his friend Haines. Both the jesting Buck Mulligan and the Anglo-Irish Haines represent a threat to Stephen and his vision of a renewed Ireland which is true to its roots. In Homeric terms, Stephen is Telemachus, the dispossessed son of Ulysses, setting off to search for his father.

In the next scene in Homer's *Odyssey*, Telemachus approaches Nestor, in the hope that he will aid him in his search. In Joyce's *Ulysses*, this is transformed into Stephen Dedalus calling on the headmaster Mr. Deasy for his wages. After this is accomplished, we follow Stephen as he walks along the strand of Dublin Bay, musing to himself as he watches the ever-changing sea. This scene parallels the Homeric Telemachus and his dealings with Proteus, the ever-changing sea god.

The parallels between *Ulysses* and Homer's *Odyssey* are far from being exact or restrictive. Joyce's intention was to make this parallel for the most part allusive, suggesting all manner of even wider resonances. Thus Stephen Dedalus does of course bear many resemblances to the young Joyce himself, just as he did in *Portait of the Artist as a Young Man*. In that earlier work, Stephen takes on certain features of Hamlet, and these are retained in *Ulysses*, with much direct emphasis and more fleeting allusion. The young Hamlet is in need of a guiding father figure, and this he will eventually find in the form of Leopold Bloom, the hero of *Ulysses*, whom we encounter in the fourth episode. The wandering Jewish figure of Bloom is

Ulysses himself, the hero of the *Odyssey*. Yet at the same time he is a distinctly ordinary man, his very ordinariness rendered heroic in the disguised mythical dangers he encounters on his wanderings through Dublin during the waking hours of June 16, 1904. Just as Joyce's father had once been, Bloom's job is soliciting advertisements for a Dublin newspaper.

We first encounter Leopold Bloom in the kitchen of his home at 7 Eccles Street, preparing breakfast for his wife Molly, who is still upstairs in bed.

Mr. Leopold Bloom ate with relish the inner organs of beasts and fowls. He liked thick giblet soup, nutty gizzards, a stuffed roast heart, liver slices fried with crustcrumbs, fried hencod's roes. Most of all he liked grilled mutton kidneys which gave to his palate a fine tang of faintly scented urine.

Kidneys were in his mind as he moved about the kitchen softly, righting her breakfast things on the humpy tray. Gelid light and air were in the kitchen but out of doors gentle summer morning everywhere. Made him feel a bit peckish.

As the book progresses, there is less emphasis upon interior monologue. In the above scene, the opening lines are undeniably third-person narrative, but their emphasis is suggestive of Bloom's character, lovingly evoking the inner organs he so relishes, the sensuality of detail indicating the man himself.

In this way Joyce manages at all times to suggest both the character and his mind, weaving in his allusions, leitmotif themes, nudging us toward his symbolism. Stephen and Bloom are very different characters, and this is immediately clear from their interior monologues. Stephen is intellectual, meditative, his vocabulary more extensive, more exotic, and more skillfully employed. He is the tyro writer who will one day become Joyce, the author of *Ulysses*. Here he is still on the Strand, watching the tide coming in:

> In long lassoes from the Cock lake the water flowed full, covering greengoldenly lagoons of sand, rising, flowing. My ashplant will

float away. I shall wait. No, they will pass on, passing chafing against the low rocks, swirling, passing. Better get this job over quickly. Listen: a fourworded wavespeech: seesoo, hrss, rsseeiss, ooos. Vehement breath of waters amid seasnakes, rearing horses, rocks. In the cups of rocks it slops: flop, slop, slap: bounded in barrels.

Bloom, on the other hand, has a more rapid-fire inner monologue, to match the outward attentiveness of his mind. He sees, he comments, he calculates, his mind entering deeply into his surroundings:

He passed Saint Joseph's, National school. Brats' clamour. Windows open. Fresh air helps memory. Or a lilt. Ahbeesee defeegee kelomen opeecue rustyouvee double you. Boys are they? Yes. Inishturk. Inishark. Inishboffin. At their joggerfry.

The children's alphabet. The islands off the west coast of Ireland, geography . . . Joyce is able to vary his interior monologues, subtly altering the depth of consciousness as it flows. Sometimes the monologuist's interest is focused upon the outside world, the passing surroundings of city life in Dublin. At other times the monologue submerges in its own inner preoccupations. This latter is always in danger of becoming opaque to the reader, as in this example from Bloom:

> A cloud began to cover the sun wholly slowly wholly. Grey. Far.
>
> No, not like that. A barren land, bare waste. Vulcanic lake, the dead sea: no fish, weedless, sunk deep in the earth. No wind would lift those waves, grey metal, poisonous foggy waters. Brimstone they called it raining down: the cities of the plain: Sodom, Gomorrah, Edom. All dead names. A dead sea in a dead land, grey and old. Old now. It bore the oldest, the first race. A bent hag crossed from Cassidy's clutching a noggin bottle by the neck. The oldest people.

Such passages should be read for their allusions, which carry us along on a tide of ever-dissolving, ever-echoing glimpses of meaning. This is the knack of finding one's way into what Joyce is saying. The greyness of overclouded Dublin becomes a meditation on the Dead Sea, God's destruction of Sodom, the land of Israel from which Bloom's people originated, the first people on earth, thus the oldest people—which thought comically coincides with Bloom's sighting of the old crone leaving the pub with her bottle.

Further into the book, *Ulysses* devolves into all manner of styles, each literally and metaphorically adapted to its place in the overall scheme of the work. These include a scene laid out as dramatic script, suggestive of the hallucinatory darkness and voices of Dublin's Nighttown and the inhabitants of its streets: the drunks, the redcoated soldiers, and the whores:

THE NAVVY: (*belching*) Where's the bloody house?

THE SHEBEENKEEPER: Purdon Street. Shilling a bottle of stout. Respectable woman.

THE NAVVY: (*gripping the two redcoats, staggers forward with them*) Come on, you British army!

PRIVATE CARR: (*behind his back*) He aint half balmy.

PRIVATE COMPTON: (*laughs*) What ho!

PRIVATE CARR: (To the navvy) Portobello Barracks canteen. You ask for Carr. Just Carr.

THE NAVVY: (*shouts*) We are the boys of Wexford.

Other scenes exhibit a cornucopia of styles, ranging from the give-and-take of Dublin bar repartee to the matter-of-fact reportage of a court circular which wittily, and then insultingly, transforms itself into the scene all around what it is describing:

William Humble, earl of Dudley, and Lady Dudley, accompanied by lieutenantcolonel Hesseltine, drove out after luncheon from the viceregal lodge. . . . The cavalcade passed out by the lower gate of Phoenix Park saluted by the obsequious policeman. . . . Between Queen's and Whitworth bridges Lord Dudley's viceregal carriages passed and were unsaluted by Mr. Dudley White, B.L., M.A., who stood on Arran Quay outside Mrs.

M. E. White's, the pawnbroker's, at the corner of Arran Street stroking his nose with his forefinger. . . . From its sluice in Wood Quay wall under Tom Devan's office Poddle river hung out in a fealty tongue of liquid sewage. . . .

Joyce intended to create not only the happenings of an exact day in Dublin, but the city itself in all its precisely named particularity. Indeed, he boasted that if Dublin should ever be destroyed, it could be reconstructed from the pages of his novel. So too could the stylistic usages of the English language. One of the later scenes is even reduced to the pedantic formal precision of a questionnaire:

What did Bloom see on the range?
    On the right (smaller) hob a blue enamelled saucepan: on the left (larger) hob a black iron kettle.

What did Bloom do at the range?
    He removed the saucepan to the left hob, rose and carried the iron kettle to the sink in

70

order to tap the current by turning the faucet to let it flow.

Did it flow?

Yes. From Roundwood reservoir in county Wicklow of a cubic capacity of 2,400 million gallons, percolating through a subterranean aqueduct of filter mains of single and double pipeage. . . .

This style cunningly reflects the ambiance of the scene, in which a drunk Stephen is sitting in the more sober Bloom's kitchen. The disjointedness is an apt indication of the difference between them. It also serves to focus the mind of the reader (as Stephen attempts to focus his own mind) after the drunkenness of the preceding scene.

By this stage at the end of the novel, Stephen (Telemachus) has been united with his father figure Bloom (Ulysses). During the long preceding action of the day their paths have occasionally crossed, but it is not until they come together in Nighttown that the significant encounter occurs, whereupon Bloom takes the drunken Stephen

71

back to his home at 7 Eccles Street. As with so much of Joyce's writing, this too has its origin in fact. Here Bloom was acting out the role of Joyce's Jewish acquaintance Alfred Hunter, who had looked after him following the fight over a girl in St. Stephen's Green. But in *Ulysses* this scene was combined with another factual incident, the occasion when Joyce got drunk after hearing gossip that Nora had betrayed him, and had been assisted by John Byrne back to his home. At the time, John Byrne was living at 7 Eccles Street.

So the wandering Ulysses (Bloom) has finally arrived home, while upstairs his wife Molly is lying in bed. Molly is a professional singer, and as wife to Bloom she is also Penelope, the wife of Ulysses. Molly's maiden name is Tweedy, particularly suggestive of Penelope, who spent her time weaving as she waited for Ulysses to return. But Molly has not remained faithful to her Ulysses. During the day she has betrayed Bloom by making love with the lecherous theatrical impresario Blazes Boyland. Here we see more of Joyce's interweaving of fact into his fiction. According to

Dublin gossip of the period, Joyce's Jewish acquaintance Alfred Hunter had an unfaithful wife. Also, in Joyce's mind the scene when he was taken back to 7 Eccles Street by Byrne was forever associated with the gossip about Nora betraying him. Although *Ulysses* was rich in literary illusions, stylistic flourishes, and other distancing devices, it remained equally rich in personal resonances for its author. As ever, Joyce's work remained deeply subjective at the same time it was formally objective. It is this combination that enabled Joyce to invest his disparate work with such constant intensity.

These apparently contradictory themes—Molly's betrayal and her symbolic role as the faithful Penelope—are eventually drawn together and resolved in her final stream of consciousness, the monologue of the voice in her mind as she lies awake in bed at Eccles Street, with Bloom at last lying asleep beside her. It is this long, flowing, punctuationless monologue that finally brings the book to its close. Molly finds herself remembering her childhood in Gibraltar, Bloom kissing her on Howth Head outside Dublin, and the first time she made love. It is evident from the rhythm of her monologue that she is at the same time masturbating, and as she relives her reveries she reaches her climax in an ultimate affirmation:

> . . . I put my arms around him yes and drew him down to me so he could feel my breasts all perfume yes and his heart was going like mad and yes I said yes I will Yes.

This is Molly's symbolic reunion and reconciliation. In her mind and in her being she is no longer unfaithful to Bloom: Penelope is rendered faithful to her returning Ulysses.

With the publication of *Ulysses* in Paris, Joyce became the foremost figure on the avant-garde literary scene. But the critics, even some of those in favor of modernism, remained divided. *Ulysses* may have been brilliant, but was it worth the effort of plowing through it? Indeed, was it readable at all? And did we really need to have all this obscenity paraded before our eyes? *Ulysses* appeared to be the product of a guttersnipe rather than a literary genius. The leading English novelist Virginia Woolf, the literary star of the Bloomsbury set, was not only repelled by the book but completely misjudged its author. For her, *Ulysses* was "the work of a self-taught working man," reminding her of "a queasy undergraduate scratching his pimples." On the other hand, the poet T. S. Eliot, who had recently published his own modernist masterpiece *The Waste Land*, was overcome with admiration, declaring: "How could anyone write again after achieving the immense prodigality of the last chapter?" Many saw the influence of Freud in Joyce's work, an influence he denied. Freud's great adversary Jung was particularly scathing about *Ulysses*, commenting that it could be read as easily backward as forward. In fact, Jung insisted, it was nothing more than an exemplary expression of a schizophrenic mind. Puzzled by the vehemence of Jung's criticism, Joyce mentioned this to a friend, who helpfully pointed out: "There can only be one explanation. Translate your name into German." (Freud means joy in German.)

It is customary on such occasions to declare that only time would tell which of these contradictory opinions would prevail. A mark of *Ulysses*'s continuing ability to excite and divide can be seen in the fact that now, more than eighty years later, Joyce's book continues to provoke strong opinions for and against, even among informed literary circles. Not until 1934, twelve years after its original publication, would a first edition of *Ulysses* be publicly published in America, with its publication in Britain having to wait another two years.

But by this time Joyce was faced with a new, seemingly intractable problem. During the early 1930s it became increasingly apparent that the behavior of his daughter Lucia was more than just that of an eccentric intellectual young woman. It was now recognized that she was mentally ill. Joyce began consulting a series of doctors, all to no avail. Eventually, despite Jung's earlier insults, he sent Lucia to him for a consultation. Jung could do little to help, but he commented perceptively to Joyce: "You are like two people going to the bottom of a river, but whereas she is drowning you are diving."

Lucia's consultations were paid for by Joyce's benefactor Harriet Weaver. Writing to thank her, Joyce vowed that he would never allow Lucia to

JAMES JOYCE'S LIFE AND WORKS

be locked up in a "mental prison." Harriet Weaver now offered to look after Lucia, who traveled to England to stay with her. But it soon became clear that Lucia's hysteria was becoming uncontrollable and dangerous, with the result that she was confined to a mental institution outside Paris.

As if this was not bad enough, Joyce's eyes had by now deteriorated to the point where he could barely see. Occasionally he was reduced to total blindness. As a result he underwent a series of operations, which also had to be "subsidized" by the long-suffering Harriet Weaver. By the 1930s she had spent almost £25,000 on Joyce, a colossal sum when a skilled workingman's wage was less than £5 a week. But not all this money was used on medical bills for Joyce and his daughter. Overcome by his sufferings and his feelings of guilt, Joyce began to inflict further sufferings on those around him. Always a heavy drinker, he proceeded to hit the bottle in an even more determined fashion. Yet he always managed to work every day. Even when blind, he dictated. But when his day's work was over, he threw all caution to the winds and drowned his sorrows. Nora soon found that she had endured more than she could take of his "tumbling about every night" when he returned in the early hours. On more than one occasion she walked out on him, eventually persuaded by Joyce's friends to return.

Nora was tough enough to look after herself; Joyce was not. He depended upon her utterly. He also loved her. In 1931 they had traveled to London and got married at the Kensington Registry Office in London. This sacrifice of Joyce's precious principles had ostensibly been because he had wished to secure for Nora the legal inheritance of his works. Another factor had been Lucia, whose psychological disturbance was not helped by her self-consciousness over her illegitimacy.

Meanwhile, isolated from the world by his purblindness, his drunkenness, his guilt, and his suffering, Joyce continued with his work. How could he progress beyond the stylistic superlatives, linguistic subtleties, and literary legerdemain of *Ulysses*? Where was he to go from here with language whose every possibility he had already explored?

The answer soon became clear to him. He had reduced language to its fundamental elements and had combined them in all manner of ways, like the atoms and molecules of the periodic table. The only way left appeared to be to split the atom of the word, thus releasing all the vast energy of its different syllabic meanings and associations. And this he did, in no uncertain fashion. The book that Joyce now set about writing was *Finnegans Wake*. This vast, all but impenetrable work is widely regarded as an aberration of genius. It would perhaps be of little more than psychological interest but for the fact that it was Joyce's inimitable genius that was involved. Aberration it may have been, but this was the ultimate literary incarnation of Shame's Voice—as Joyce punningly referred to himself (or Germ's Choice, as a wicked parodist would have it).

The supreme difficulties of *Finnegans Wake* are glaringly apparent from the opening lines:

riverrun, past Eve and Adam's, from swerve of shore to bend of bay, brings us to a commodius vicus of recirculation back to Howth Castle and Environs.

Sir Tristram, violer d'amores, fr'over the short sea, had passencore rearrived from North America on this side. . . .

What on earth does all this mean? Bear in mind that Joyce was almost blind at the time of writing this work. Pay less attention to the normal surface of meaning and the visual associations. Instead, listen to the language, to the glimmers and associations compressed within his words and their echoes, which can be more easily released when we concentrate upon the sounds of the words. According to Joyce, "It is all so simple. If anyone doesn't understand a passage, all he need do is read it aloud." But remember that these words are being spoken in an Irish accent, more particularly a Dublin accent. This accent has on occasion been claimed as the purest of all English accents, whatever that means. But it certainly makes some distinctions which are not apparent in other pronunciations. For instance, it is capable of elucidating both the "t" and the "h" in "the"—a feat that eludes all but a few Irish accents.

This is literature as puzzle. Yet for those who consider the effort worth it, the puzzle is enriched by the humor, the poetry, and the sheer playfulness of ingenuity involved. So what precisely does the puzzle of those opening lines yield? The opening half-sentence gives the book its circularity: it is the second half of the sentence that ends the work. The river is Dublin's river Liffey, which in fact runs past the church of Adam and Eve. Joyce reverses this to imply one of the many themes of the book, which is temptation (by Eve), fall (Adam's), and renewal. This also asscociates Dublin with the Garden of Eden. The river runs through the city, out around Dublin Bay to Howth, the north of the bay, with its castle. Howth Castle and Environs introduces the letters H C E, which are the initials of the central character, H. C. Earwicker, which stand for Here Comes Everybody, alluding to his universal character. . . . And this is just the beginning of *an* explanation of the opening lines of the book!

On the simplest level, *Finnegans Wake* is the dream of the publican H. C. Earwicker, who runs an establishment in Chapelizod (where Joyce's father had once worked). H C E becomes both the city of Dublin and all male humanity. The complementary female principle is his wife Anna Livia Plurabelle, the river Liffey, which flows down from the mountains, through the city of Dublin, into Dublin Bay where she is absorbed by the sea (and then rises as vapor to condense into a cloud, which falls as rain over the mountains, to complete the circularity). Another aspect of circularity and renewal is present in the title *Finnegans Wake*. This derives from an American-Irish ballad about the whiskey-loving Tim Finnegan who falls off a ladder and is killed. At his riotous wake, whiskey is accidentally splattered over his body, whereupon he revives.

Finnegans Wake is filled with punny jokes and hokey fun. They spill into more than forty languages, ranging from pun-European to Aleasiatic, on through Norse, Erse, and Burmese. All this serves to give the text different strata of meaning, which resonate with one another. We may be more used to literature consisting of one literal layer of meaning, which may have symbolic resonances, or even allude to a parallel allegorical level of meaning. But such is the complexity of *Finnegans Wake* that we are not only forced to abandon our habitual notions of meaning but also our preconceived notions of reading. In the attempt to gain access to the meanings, echo-meanings, and allusions of Joyce's prose, we are forced to immerse ourselves in the text as a flow of words rather than build up the meaning of each sentence, word by word: "leaning with the sloothering slide of her, giddy-gaddy, grannyma, gossipaceous Anna Livia."

Finnegans Wake was initially issued in episodes—such as "Anna Livia Plurabelle" and "Haveth Childers Everywhere"—under the collective title of *Work in Progress*. The actual title was not to be revealed until the completed work was published in 1939. By this time even the initial episodes had been "condensed" so as to thicken the text into an even more complex surface of punnillusions and neologorrhea.

First reviewers were predictably baffled. The literary critic of London's *Daily Herald* dismissed the work in a single sentence as "An Irish stew of verbiage by the author of *Ulysses* with unexpected beauty emerging now and then from the peculiar mixture." Oliver St. John Gogarty referred to it as "the most colossal leg pull in literature," and even Joyce's tireless sponsor Harriet Weaver was disappointed. But Joyce had now begun to appeal to a new generation, and the coming Irish writer Samuel Beckett perceptively declared that Joyce's writing in *Finnegans Wake* "is not *about* something; *it is that something itself.*" Beckett had left provincial Dublin to take up residence in Paris for many of the same reasons as Joyce, and the two had soon become friends. When Joyce's eyes had become too afflicted, Beckett had taken Joyce's dictation of passages that went into *Finnegans Wake*—a feat involving considerable empathy and understanding.

By the time *Finnegans Wake* was published in 1939, Joyce was ill and aged beyond his fifty-seven years. In the same year Europe plunged

84

into the Second World War—a cause of further suffering for Joyce, who complained that now no one would have time to spend reading and working out all that lay hidden in the pages of *Finnegans Wake*. When the Nazis invaded France in 1940, he and Nora fled back to Zurich in neutral Switzerland. But the strain of the journey and the fact that once again he found himself penniless in another foreign country was all too much for Joyce. He fell seriously ill with an ulcer and died within a matter of weeks on January 13, 1941.

Afterword

Nora was left impoverished by Joyce's death, but friends sent her what money they could. She still refrained from reading Joyce's work but proudly insisted to everyone she met that she had been married to the world's greatest writer. Although her circumstances eventually improved with the arrival of postwar royalties, she was bored without Joyce: "There was always something to do when he was about." When the Irish government refused to allow Joyce to be reburied in Ireland (where his works were still banned as obscene), Nora retaliated by refusing to allow them the manuscript of *Finnegans Wake*, selling it instead to the British Library. She died just ten years after

Joyce, in 1951. In the ensuing decades, Beckett tried to have Joyce's remains reinterred in the city where they belonged. Today Bloomsday is marked by annual celebrations in Dublin while Joyce and Nora remain buried side by side, still in exile, in Switzerland.

When *Ulysses* was published in 1922, few regarded it as a masterpiece. Even among those who had greeted it favorably, many were of the opinion that such an "odd" book would not last much beyond its time. Within a few years, however, Joyce's stylistic innovations were beginning to crop up in the works of a wide range of writers. Most of them sought to absorb Joyce's ambitious and experimental flights of style into a more acceptable and mainstream form. Again, the feeling was that such an "unreadable" work as *Ulysses* could not continue to appeal to any wider audience, even among the most educated readers. Its legacy would be one of influence and absorbtion: transforming the prose of those who came after it. The book itself would gradually recede into the background, treasured only by the cognoscenti.

As it happened, nothing was farther from the truth. The close of the twentieth century brought the inevitable polls for the "book of the century," and to the surprise of many *Ulysses* topped poll after poll. Not everyone had managed to read all the way through this difficult work, but there was a considerable body of readers who recognized its unassailable greatness. *Ulysses*, which attempted to be the book of one particular summer's day in a particular provincial city, had grown in stature to be acclaimed as the work that most character-ized twentieth-century literature throughout the world.

Likewise, when polls are held to choose the greatest short stories ever written, Joyce's "The Dead," the final long story in *Dubliners*, regu-larly appears among the top ten, alongside such masters as Tolstoy, Chekhov, and de Maupas-sant. In "The Dead," many felt that Joyce had created a consummate example of this difficult form.

And what of *Finnegans Wake*? Joyce's final work remains for all and sundry as difficult and impenetrable as ever. Yet this very quality has drawn to it a small but persistent high intellectual audience. Few but determined are the minds that have been willing to seek their relaxation in puzzling out the jests and idiosyncracies of Joyce's labyrinthine mind. *Finnegans Wake* has come to be regarded as a cult work for gifted connoisseurs. Joyce himself promised that it would take a lifetime of dedicated study for the reader to appreciate and understand this work, and some have been willing to answer his call.

One unforeseen result of this exacting study is that *Finnegans Wake* has entered the language of science. The Nobel prize–winning American particle physicist and amateur multilinguist Murray Gell-Mann delighted in spending hours poring over *Finnegans Wake*. When, in the course of his scientific work, he discovered a new class of subatomic particles, he decided to name it after the following passage:

> —*Three quarks for Muster Mark!*
> *Sure he hasn't got much of a bark.*
> *And sure as any he has it's all beside the mark.*

This is the origin of the name "quark" for a certain class of subatomic particles. Even Joyce himself might have been surprised at his achievement of immortality in the realm of nuclear physics!

From James Joyce's Writings

Taken from the early childhood section of Portrait of the Artist as a Young Man, *this scene depicts Stephen Dedalus playing a reluctant role on the playing fields of Clongowes Wood College:*

The wide playgrounds were swarming with boys. All were shouting and the prefects urged them on with strong cries. The evening air was pale and chilly and after every charge and thud of the footballers the greasy leather orb flew like a heavy bird through the grey light. He kept on the fringe of his line, out of sight of his prefect, out of the reach of the rude feet, feigning to run now and then. He felt his body small and weak amid the throng of players and his eyes were weak and watery. Rody Kickham was not like that: he would be captain of the third line all the fellows said.

Rody Kickham was a decent fellow but Nasty Roche was a stink. Rody Kickham had greaves in his number and a hamper in the refectory. Nasty Roche had big hands. He called the Friday pudding dog-in-the-blanket.

The Jesuit priest Father Arnall describes the fires of hell in his sermon during the retreat attended by Stephen Dedalus in Portrait of the Artist as a Young Man:

. . . the strength and quality and boundlessness of this fire is as nothing when compared to its intensity, an intensity which it has as being the instrument chosen by divine design for the punishment of soul and body alike. It is a fire which proceeds directly from the ire of God, working not of its own activity but as an instrument of divine vengeance. As the waters of baptism cleanse the soul with the body so do the fires of punishment torture the spirit with the flesh. Every sense of the flesh is tortured and every faculty of the soul therewith: the eyes with impenetrable utter darkness, the nose with noisome odours, the ears with yells and howls and execrations, the taste with foul matter, leprous corruption, nameless suffocating filth, the touch with redhot goads and spikes, with cruel tongues of flame. And through the several torments of the senses the immortal soul is tortured eternally in its very essense amid the leagues upon leagues of glowing fires kindled in the abyss by the offended majesty of the Omnipotent God and fanned into everlasting and everincreasing fury by the breath of the anger of the Godhead.

Here, in the opening scene of Ulysses, *we inhabit the consciousness of Stephen Dedalus, following the associations of his thought, when the milkwoman arrives at the Martello Tower on her morning round. Making use of the drift of Stephen's thoughts, Joyce indicates the Homeric substructure upon which his* Ulysses *is based, identifying the milkwoman as Mentor:*

He watched her pour into the measure and thence into the jug rich white milk, not hers. Old shrunken paps. She poured again a measureful and a tilly. Old and secret she had entered from a morning world, maybe a messenger. She praised the goodness of the milk, pouring it out. Crouching by a patient cow at daybreak in the lush field, a witch on her toadstool, her wrinkled fingers quick at the squirting dugs. They lowed about her whom they knew, dewsilky cattle. Silk of the kine and poor old woman, names given her in old times. A wandering crone, lowly form of an immortal serving her conqueror and her gay betrayer, their common cuckquean, a messenger from the secret morning. To serve or to upbraid, whether he could not tell: but scorned to beg her favour.

The scene toward the end of Ulysses *after the eventual meeting of Stephen Dedalus and*

Leopold Bloom, the latter acting as a good samaritan to the drunken Stephen:

Preparatory to anything else Mr Bloom brushed off the greater bulk of the shavings and handed Stephen the hat and ashplant and bucked him up generally in the orthodox Samaritan fashion, which he very badly needed. His (Stephen's) mind was not exactly what you would call wandering but a bit unsteady and on his expressed desire for some beverage to drink Mr Bloom, in view of the hour it was and there being no pumps of Vartry water available for their ablutions, let alone drinking purposes, hit upon an expedient by suggesting, off the reel, the propriety of the cabman's shelter, as it was called, hardly a stonesthrow away near Butt Bridge, where they might hit upon some drinkables in the shape of a milk and soda or a mineral. But how to get there was the rub.

The final passage of Ulysses, *which conveys the stream of consciousness of Molly Bloom lying in bed as she approaches her climax and symbolic reconciliation with her husband Leopold Bloom in an ultimate affirmation:*

. . . O and the sea the sea crimson sometimes like fire and the glorious sunsets and the figtrees in the Almeda gardens yes and all the queer little streets and pink and blue and yellow houses and the rosegardens and the jessamine and geraniums and cactuses and Gibraltar as a girl where I was a flower of the mountain yes when I put the rose in my hair like the Andalusian girls used or shall I wear a red yes and how he kissed me under the Moorish wall and I thought well as well him as another and then I asked him with my eyes to ask again yes and then he asked me would I yes to say yes my mountain flower and first I put my arms around him yes and drew him down to me so he could feel my breasts all perfume yes and his heart was going like mad and yes I said yes I will Yes.

The clebrated Anna Livia Plurabelle passage from Finnegans Wake, *which starts from the source of*

the River Liffey, the female principle who comple-
ments her husband H. C. Earwicker (Here Comes
Everybody):

O

tell me all about

Anna Livia! I want to hear all

about Anna Livia. Well, you know Anna Livia?
Yes, of course, we all know Anna Livia. Tell me
all. Tell me now. You'll die when you hear. Well,
you know, when the old cheb went futt and did
what you know. Yes, I know, go on. Wash quit
and don't be dabbling. Tuck up your sleeves and
loosen your talktapes. And don't butt me—
hike!—when you bend. Or whatever it was they
threed to make out he thried to two in the
Fiendish park.

A duzany shortle Choicisms (or A dozen short
Joycisms):

—Shame's Voice. Jeems Jokes.
—The snotgreen sea. The scrotumtightening sea.
—Agenbite of inwit.

—*Three quarks for Muster Mark!*

—When I was Jung and easily Freudened.

—World's greatest shopping hour (Schopenhauer).

—The Devil mostly speaks a language called Bellsybabble.

—Ireland is the old sow that eats her farrow.

—When I makes tea I makes tea, as old mother Grogan said. And when I makes water I makes water.

—Rutland blue's gone out of passion.

—History, Stephen said, is a nightmare from which I am trying to awake.

—A face as long as a late breakfast.

James Joyce's Chief Works

Chamber Music (1907)
Dubliners (1914)*†
Portrait of the Artist as a Young Man (1916)*†
Exiles (1918)
Ulysses (1922)*†
Pomes Penyeach (1927)
Finnegans Wake (1939)*†

*major works
†discussed in text

Chronology of James Joyce's Life and Times

1882   James Joyce born on February 2 at
        Rathgar, Dublin, in Ireland, then part of
        the British Isles.

1888   Joyce sent as boarder to prestigous
        Clongowes Wood College.

1893   Goes to Belvedere College in Dublin.

1895   Trial and imprisonment of Oscar Wilde
        on charges of homosexuality.

1899   Enters University College, Dublin.

1900   Publication of Joyce's article on Ibsen in
        the *Fortnightly Review.*

1901   Death of Queen Victoria.

1902   Joyce travels to Paris.

1903   Returns from Paris. Death of Joyce's
        mother.

1904   Joyce meets Nora Barnacle. "Bloomsday,"
        June 16, day he first goes out with Nora.
        Joyce elopes with Nora to Pola, on the
        Adriatic, where he teaches English at the
        Berlitz School.

1905   Moves to Trieste. Birth of his son Giorgio.
        Joyce joined by brother Stanislaus in
        Trieste.

1906   Birth of Samuel Beckett. Death of Ibsen.

1907   Daughter Lucia born.

1909   Joyce returns to Ireland with aim of
        setting up a string of cinemas in Dublin,
        Cork, and Belfast. Volta cinema in Dublin
        opens briefly, then folds.

1914   Serialization of *Portrait of the Artist as a
        Young Man* in *The Egoist* magazine.
        Publication of *Dubliners*. Outbreak of
        First World War. Irish Home Rule Bill
        passed but not enacted on account of war.

1915   Joyce moves with family to Zurich in
        neutral Switzerland.

1916   Easter Rising in Dublin. Dadaist
        movement founded in Zurich.

1917   Bolshevik Revolution brings Lenin and the
        Communists to power in Russia.

1918   End of First World War. Irish rebel
        Constance Markiewicz elected first
        woman member of British Parliament.

1920   Joyce and family take up residence in
        Paris, where he will remain until the year
        before his death.

1922   Publication of *Ulysses* by Sylvia Beach's
        Shakespeare & Company in Paris. *Annus
        mirabilis* of modernism, with publication
        of *Ulysses*, Eliot's *The Waste Land*,
        Wittgenstein's *Tractatus Logico-
        Philosophicus,* and Rilke's completion of
        his *Duino Elegies*. Ireland gains
        independence from Britain with the
        establishment of the Irish Free State (not
        including Ulster, which remains part of
        Britain). Outbreak of Irish Civil War
        between new Irish government and
        extreme Republicans (ends 1923).

1923   W. B. Yeats wins Nobel Prize for
        Literature.

1926   George Bernard Shaw wins Nobel Prize
        for Literature.

1927   Joyce publishes *Pomes Penyeach*.

1929   Wall Street crash precipitates worldwide
        Great Depression. First "talkies" in
        motion pictures. Baird demonstrates early
        television. Publication of *Our
        Exagmination* . . . essays on *Work in
        Progress* (which became *Finnegans Wake*).

1931   Joyce and Nora Barnacle are married at
        Kensington Registry office in London, to
        secure her inheritance of Joyce's works.

1932   Lucia Joyce diagnosed mentally unstable.

1933   Hitler and the Nazis come to power in
        Germany.

1936   *Ulysses* published in Britain.

1939   Death of W. B. Yeats. Birth of Seamus
        Heaney. Outbreak of Second World War in
        Europe. Publication of *Finnegans Wake*.

1940   In December, Joyce moves to Zurich in
        neutral Switzerland.

1941   In January, Joyce dies in Zurich at age
        fifty-nine.

Recommended Reading

Anthony Burgess, *Here Comes Everybody: An Intro-
duction to James Joyce for the Ordinary Reader*
(Hamlyn, 1982). An excellent no-nonsense guide
to Joyce and his works by a sympathetic fellow
writer. As Burgess says, "I do not pretend to schol-
arship, only a desire to help the average reader."

Joseph Campbell, *A Skeleton Key to Finnegans Wake*
(Viking, 1986). A brave attempt to unravel the
unfathomable mysteries of *Finnegans Wake*:
"Like a millrace it sweeps down and out of sight,
to strike again the paddle wheel of revolving
time. As the dark torrent disappears from view,
we are left standing on the bank, bewildered, yet
strangley refreshed by the passage of these mirac-
ulous waters."

Stan Gébler Davies, *James Joyce: A Portrait of the Artist* (Stein and Day, 1975). A shorter, more amenable biography which can be read like a novel. This is both more speculative and less reticent than the definitive Ellman. Joyce's sexual life, his fondness for Swiss wine (Fendant de Sion), his constant borrowings and bickerings— all this and much more are woven into an endlessly entertaining narrative. Gébler also has the advantage of being a Dubliner.

Richard Ellman, *James Joyce* (Oxford University Press, 1983). This is the definitive biography of Joyce, a labor of love covering almost nine hundred pages. It records the life of Joyce in considerable detail, quoting from letters and contemporaries; on top of this it also examines the works and their sources. Ellman immersed himself in Joyce, his works, and all manner of Joyceana. If you want to know where in Zurich Joyce's friend pawned a gold watch in order to raise money for the impecunious author, this is the place to look.

Richard Ellman, ed., *Selected Letters of James Joyce* (Faber and Faber, 1975). A comprehensive selection, covering everything from his early missives to Nora Barnacle to his last postcard from Zurich to his brother Stanislaus. Joyce could be a tricky and skittish letter writer but was seldom confessional. Despite this, the brilliant but difficult character of "Shame's Voice" shines through in almost every line.

Stuart Gilbert, *James Joyce's Ulysses* (Vintage, 1955). An exhaustive study of *Ulysses*, penetrating many of its obscurities and throwing light on the novel's inner structure, its symbolism, and its many Dublin references.

Our Exagmination Round His Factification for Incamination of Work in Progress by Samuel Beckett and Others (Faber and Faber, 1972). This work contains essays by various authors and friends of Joyce, including as well as Beckett the poet William Carlos Williams and Robert McAlmon. The "Work in Progress" of the title would eventually become *Finnegans Wake*, and these essays were intended to prepare the way for the wider publication of this extremely difficult work, which was beginning to appear in installments in the magazine *transition*. For those who find *Finnegans Wake* all a bit too much, there are also appended "Two Letters of Protest," one in the form of an amusing parody by Vladimir Dixon addressed to "Germs Choice."

RECOMMENDED READING

Edmund Wilson, *Axel's Castle: A Study of the Imaginative Literature of 1870–1930* (Farrar, Straus and Giroux, 2004). This work by the great American literary critic of the twentieth century places Joyce's work in the context of modernism, from Rimbaud to T. S. Eliot by way of Gertrude Stein and Paul Valéry.

Index

A NOTE ON THE AUTHOR

Paul Strathern has lectured in philosophy and mathematics and now lives and writes in London. He is the author of the enormously successful series Philosophers in 90 Minutes. A Somerset Maugham Prize winner, he is also the author of books on history and travel, as well as five novels. His articles have appeared in a great many publications, including the *Observer* (London) and the *Irish Times*.

Paul Strathern's 90 Minutes series in philosophy, also published by Ivan R. Dee, includes individual books on Thomas Aquinas, Aristotle, St. Augustine, Berkeley, Confucius, Derrida, Descartes, Dewey, Foucault, Hegel, Heidegger, Hume, Kant, Kierkegaard, Leibniz, Locke, Machiavelli, Mars, J. S. Mill, Nietzsche, Plato, Rousseau, Bertrand Russell, Sartre, Schopenhauer, Socrates, Spinoza, and Wittgenstein.